I0136841

Thomas Lister

A Mirror for Princes

In a letter to His Royal Highness the Prince of Wales

Thomas Lister

A Mirror for Princes
In a letter to His Royal Highness the Prince of Wales

ISBN/EAN: 9783337329310

Printed in Europe, USA, Canada, Australia, Japan

Cover: Foto ©ninafisch / pixelio.de

More available books at **www.hansebooks.com**

A

MIRROR FOR PRINCES,

IN A

LETTER

TO HIS ROYAL HIGHNESS THE

PRINCE OF WALES.

By HAMPDEN.

In commune jubes fi quid, cenfefve tenendum
Primus juffa fubi : Tunc obfervantior æqui
Fit Popu'us ; nec ferre negat, cum viderit ipfum
Auctorem parere fibi.   Componitur orbis
Regis ad exemplum : Nec fic inflectere fenfus
Humanos Edicta valent, ac Vita regentis.

CLAUDIAN : de 4to. Confulat : Honorii;

LONDON:

PRINTED FOR J. S. JORDAN, NO. 166, FLEET-STREET.

MDCCXCVII.

PRINCE OF WALES.

SIR,

IN the hour of national adverſity, we involuntarily apply for protection to thoſe whom chance, cuſtom, or our own conſent, ſhall have conſtituted our governors.—If there is any time in which the relative ſituations and dependencies of the governors and the governed are peculiarly felt and underſtood, it is in ſuch a ſeaſon of general calamity— It is then we anxiouſly preſs forward to thoſe Authorities in whom we have veſted the faireſt privileges of our nature.—The com-

B   mon

mon principles of moral juſtice teach us that
it is but reaſonable to expect ſome return
from thoſe to whom nothing has been de-
nied—It is from this idea we lay aſide the
humble air of ſupplication, and approach
you with the ingenuous confidence of friend-
ſhip.—It will be a conſolation to us to learn
that our calamities proceed from any cauſe
rather than from the hand of thoſe whom we
have cheerfully and indulgently foſtered—
We ſhould be unwilling to diſcover an ene-
my where we hoped and believed we poſſeſs-
ed a friend.—Gratifying will it be to us to be
convinced, that the ſeeds of our bounty have
not been ſcattered upon barren and inhoſpita-
ble ground : that we may not have to repeat
the Athenian reproach to the rivals and enemies of their country ;

Αλλ ατεχνωο καΊα του Αισωπε μυθον, εν ῆ αλωπηξ
πρσσ ται λεονΊα ειπε, και ἒ εισ Λακεδαμονα
νομισμαΊες
εισιονΊοσ μεντα ιχνη τα εκεισε τεΊραμμενα
δηλα, εξιόντοσ ϋδαμη αν Ίισ ιδσι.*

The

---

* That, according to the Fable of Æſop, where the
Fox addreſſes the Lion, we may trace the ſteps of the good
things

The moment, Sir, is arrived when thofe to whom power and authority have been delegated ought to affure us of their ability and inclination to protect us.—It is now we may exclaim to our rulers of every defcription; " Our calamities are no longer to be con-
" cealed.—Knowing a good government to
" be neceffary for the happinefs of the peo-
" ple, and the happinefs of the people to be
" the only true principle on which a good
" government can be founded, we have fur-
" veyed our conftitution with the fondeft
" admiration—We have intrufted it to your
" hands as a facred depofit in which every
" thing deareft to us was involved—How
" fincerely we have fubmitted to the high
" authority you have derived from fo import-
" ant a charge, our conduct has manifefted—
" You have promulgated Laws and we have
" obeyed them; you have demanded money
" to an enormous amount and we have grant-
" ed it; you have rioted in luxury and we
" have forborne to envy you; you have been

---

things going into Lacedemon, but cannot d fcover any marks of their return.

PLATO Alcibia. Prim.

" amufed

" amufed with diftinctions, and we have be-
" held them with filent indifference. —
" Having received your wages, we doubt
" not you have performed your fervice, at
" leaft, we have a right to expect it.—When
" misfortunes opprefs us, we naturally fly
" for a refuge to the guardians of that con-
" ftitution which was formed for the pre-
" fervation of our happinefs—we fhould be
" loath to fufpect that you have abufed the
" confidence we have repofed in you, and
" that you have returned our kindnefs with
" ingratitude ; that you have been negligent
" and inattentive to our welfare.—The op-
" portunity is now offered you of afferting
" your integrity, and proving to us that you
" have not taken advantage of our honeft
" and unfufpecting attachment—But the fim-
" plicity of our nature may perhaps encou-
" rage us to be too fanguine. Let us, for a
" moment, reprefs the ardour of our hopes,
" let us cautioufly examine in whom we may
" confide, let us learn to diftinguifh thofe
" who have confcientioufly performed their
" truft, from the men whom we are in future
                                    " to

" to regard as the abandoned and unprinci-
" pled betrayers of our country."—Such, Sir,
it may be eafily conceived are at this moment the fentiments of the people of England.

Amidft the band of our Legiflators, you,
Sir, ftand in too confpicuous a fituation not
immediately to arreft our attention,*Εχδη-
λοσμε]α πασιν, as a Peer of Parliament, a privy
Counfellor, heir apparent to the Crown, the
the firft born amongft the adopted children
of the people, you are irrefiftibly forced upon our notice.—

You muft forgive me, Sir, if in the following pages, the uncourtly fimplicity of my
phrafe, the unftudied plainnefs of my addrefs
fhall be grating to an ear too long habituated
to the foothing, but treacherous modulations
of flattery.—If I boaft not the elegant characteriftics of the Great, I may hope for an
equal exemption from their vices.—Though
I fhall

* Confpicuous amongft the many.
HOMER's ILIAD,

I shall forbear wantonly to insult. I come
not as the minister of your pleasure—my
praises where you deserve them, shall be
without adulation, my remonstrances without bitterness.

That I may omit no circumstance tending
to illustrate your character, I shall commence
my enquiries from the earliest period of your
life.—Though you cannot explain with the
visionary Glendower,

——*At my nativity*
The front of Heaven was full of fiery shapes
Of living Cressets, and at my birth
The frame and the foundation of the world
Shak'd like a coward.——

Your entrance into the world was accom-
panied by circumstances, if of a more humble, certainly of a more gratifying nature to
your future feelings.—At your birth the
voice of honest joy vibrated on every tongue,
every heart beat with an emotion of the
liveliest pleasure.—It was something of a
paren-

parental feeling that animated the people of
England; as your political fathers, they
fondled you as the favourite child of the state
and they indulged for you (cannot Sir, be
ignorant of the proverbial partiality of parents,) the most enthusiastic hopes of your
future virtues.—I envy you Sir, the exquisite
satisfaction you must experience, if you have
the consciousness of having realized these
hopes, of having by the purity of your life,
requited their affectionate kindness.—Your
education was a subject of too great importance, to be hastily or negligently considered.
—Your supposed natural goodness of disposi-
tion was to be strengthened by every precau-
tion human sagacity could devise.—To arouse
you to wisdom and to virtue, by affording
you such means of acquiring them, as should
render your deficiency in either disgraceful,
was the spirit that animated the whole system
of your education. Your preceptors were
men of great and enlightened minds—you imbibed learning from its purest and most captivating source—He must indeed be dull of
heart to whom instruction could fail to be
de-

delightful when flowing from the mouth of the elegant and engaging Hurd—Nor were the leſſons of morality leſs advantageouſly recommended—The virtuous precepts you received from your inſtructors were inforced by the example you daily witneſſed of their practice in the domeſtic circle of your royal Parents—Such, Sir, were the advantages that attended you from the firſt dawning of your ideas, and our hopes were proportionally great—We heard with delight the progreſs of your ſtudies, and we dwelt with rapture on the encomiums paſſed on your underſtanding, your claſſical taſte, your numerous and encreaſing virtues; your preceptors (who with all their merits were courtiers indeed) might be allowed a little exaggeration in favour of their princely pupil.—But courtly politeneſs cannot exceed the bounds of popular enthuſiaſm—Had praiſes, in a tenfold greater degree been laviſhed on your merits, in the fullneſs of our hearts we ſhould have given them our ſincereſt belief. Here, Sir, let us pauſe awhile, let us awefully ponder on the inpenetrable uncertainty that envelopes the diſpoſition of

human

human affairs.—Let thofe who repofe in the
fecurity of worldly advantages; who from the
pinnacle of their pride, look infultingly down
on the unenlightened multitude, check their
pharafaical contempt and learn the leffon of
humility—Let the difciples of virtue, however lowly, however ftruggling againft the
temporary tide of adverfity, rejoice in that
purity without whofe benignant influence,
the fplendor of birth, the graces of education,
the magnificence of power become degraded
and defpifed.

Pardon, Sir this involuntary digreffion—
I will return while yet I am able, to the contemplation of your character ftill beaming
with the luftre of youthful innocence, fpot-
lefs and unfullied—We now behold you en-
tering upon the great and active Theatre of
life with a mingled fenfation of anxiety and
delight—The graces of your perfon, the
manly animation of your countenance, the
affability of your manner,* the charms of

C   your

---

* I may be accufed of trifling when I enlarge fo copioufly on
thefe external accomplifhments—but fuch qualifications are of
no

your converfation promifed the exiftence of
ftill more folid and valuable endowments—
We could not fuppofe (at leaft we would not
allow ourfelves to fuppofe) that the exterior
accomplifhments which had fo fafcinated our
attention, were but as treacherous deceptions,
by which our honeft affections were to be
enfnared and deluded—We were incapable
of fo ungenerous a fufpicion—If indeed a
flight fhade of inquietude tinctured our fatisfaction, it fprung from the fears natural to
thofe who are accuftomed to obferve the dangerous volatility of youth.—We tremblingly
prayed that you might not want the refolution
to refift the hoft of temptations we knew
would encircle you, e'er you had well ftepped
beyond the threfhold of your youthful afylum.
But when we remembered the excellence of
your education, our diftruft was extinguifhed
and we furveyed you with a confidence in your
                                    virtues

---

no ordinary account in the catalogue of princely virtues.—The
power of Elizabeth was not a little ftrengthened, and the affections of her People invigorated by the gracious condefcenfion
and dignified fweetnefs of her manner, fo that as Nat. Bacon
fays, " A Courtier might make a better meal from one good
look from her, than of a gift from fome other."

virtues which it muſt have required Hercu-
lean labour to have ſhaken.

Think not, Sir, the world ſo ſtoically rigid
in its morality, as not to make ſome allow-
ances for the warmth and vivacity of youth
—They wiſhed not to freeze the current of
your blood e'er it had well begun to flow—It
was with pleaſure they heard you acknowledged as " the glaſs of faſhion, the obſerved
of all obſervers"—They ſmiled with com-
placency on the gaiety of your equipages and
the expenſive taſte of your apparel—Your oc-
caſional ſacrifices at the ſhrine of Bacchus
excited not the indignation of a moment—
Your amours, though perhaps not always
highly creditable to your taſte, they regarded,
but as

Vi'lets in the youth of primy nature;
Sweet but not permanent.

While you ſported on the ſurface of folly they
had little apprehenſion for your ſafety—Their
partiality was yet undiminiſhed, and you ſtill
triumphed over the affections of an admiring

and

and indulgent people—Your irregularities were mingled with traits of fomething like goodnefs, of which they were willing to make the moft—They faw your name blazing at the head of benevolent fubfcriptions and patriotic inftitutions, and they augured favourably of the excellence of your heart and your attachment to the interefts of the Country—They fufpected you not of deceitful oftentation—The fimplicity natural to your years forbade them to fuppofe it.

Happy fhould I feel, Sir, if the profpect brightened as it expanded—The time was now approaching when thofe who had blindly dwelt on your imaginary excellence, ftarting from their dream of fatisfaction, waked to the bitter fenfe of your fhamelefs degradation. They could no longer acknowledge the former idol of their hopes, in the frequenter of riotous clubs, the affociate of unprincipled gamefters and mendicant patriots, the dupe of the very refufe of proftitution—Your vices had not even the pretenfions of elegance to recommend them—It was mortifying to behold the Heir apparent of the Crown dwindled to a calculator

calculator of chances. The rival of jockies, the needy dependant of jews—For fuch were the miferable fhifts to which your boundlefs extravagance had reduced you.—We have, indeed, fometimes been diverted from the groveling contemplation of your undignified pleafures by a convulfive effort of magnificent parade. You were willing, perhaps, to indulge your liberal benefactors, the generous people of England, with a fight of fomething for their money—It is with this view, no doubt, you have emerged from the obfcure fcenes of your paftime, the intemperate orgies of a tavern, or the fullen hilarity of a gaming-houfe, and have fluttered the Phœnix of a Birth-day. But I' will confefs to you, Sir, that when on fuch occafions our ears have been invaded by encomiums of your princely tafte, when the gorgeous fplendor of your ftar or your fword knot has gratified the admiring multitude, fome of us have withdrawn ourfelves from the ravifhing fpectacle. — We fear our Gothic barbarity may be cenfured; but the concentrated fplendor of the Eaft would have had but little charm for us when confidered

as

as a diminution of the fcanty fruits of the
hard and cheerlefs labour of an induftrious
people.—The brilliancy of your diamonds
might have dazzled our eyes, but could not
have fafcinated our underftanding—we might
have admired the richnefs of your jewels
and the tafte of their arrangement, but we
fhould have ftill remembered the fource from
whence you derived them.—The pomp of
the drawing-room could not have effaced
from our painful recollection the comfortlefs
habitation of the honeft artificer and opprefs-
ed peafant—we fhould have ill-reftrained an
emotion of generous indignation in beholding one man tricked out with a coftly pro-
fufion capable of affording happinefs to
ftarving thoufands, at leaft as virtuous as
himfelf.

I declaim not, Sir, againft the decent
magnificence of Royalty—I am alarmed only
by its exceffes. That the Executive Power
fhould be attended with a certain degree of
Pomp feems to have been one of the eftablifhed data in the government of every
country. It is a tacit acknowledgement of
                                    human

human frailty, a compromife between vice on the one hand and ignorance on the other, a painted veil to fcreen the irregularities and profligacy of power and to amufe and gratify the ignorance of the people.—'Till that period fhall arrive when Truth and Juftice fhall be loved merely for themfelves, 'till good Laws fhall ceafe to be degraded by the unworthinefs of thofe appointed to adminifter them, 'till the people fhall be fo inftructed as to underftand and value what is right, it is a deception not to be difpenfed with.

Your friends, or your *panegyrifts*, (for I fhall have occafion to prove in the following pages that they are by no means fynonymous terms) have dwelt with much feeming fatisfaction on the outfet of your political career ; the active part you took in oppofing the meafures of minifters, in checking the prerogative of the Crown that was fome time to be your own, evinced an independency of fpirit very grateful to the feelings of the country—there were fome, perhaps, the icy coldnefs of whofe cautious prudence was not

to

to be melted by the warm breathings of Liberty, however they might admire your magnanimity, thought lefs highly of your wifdom in endeavouring to leffen the value of your inheritance—*They* reafoned upon better grounds, who feeling for the caufe of Liberty alone, beheld with the fincereft pain your union with the forces of oppofition—They regarded it as an unnatural compact—The ftern fimplicity of independence was but an ill-forted companion for the voluptuous defcendant of Royalty.—Characters fo oppofite could not long be united without one fide partaking of the prevailing influence of the other. Our confidence in you, Sir, was too much difturbed to encourage us to believe that you would abandon the meretricious allurements of pleafure for the fober embraces of virtue, We dreaded the influence of the dazzling attractions annexed to your ftation over the honeft minds of your new affociates.—We dreaded that by diverting the polluted ftream of courtly corruption into the pure channel of public virtue, you would poifon the fources of our political

fecurity

security—For it was at that time, Sir, the people of England confided in a virtuous opposition as inseparable from the safety of the Constitution—that the fears of your deadly influence were not entirely unfounded, the event has too well proved.—As the head of a Party, your conduct stamped a character on the whole.—Those who did not actually mingle in your effeminate debaucheries, partook of something of the odium. — The opposition by ceasing to be virtuous, ceased to be respectable—it was no further to be trusted by the people—indeed their interests seemed to be the last object of consideration. It was no longer the cause of the people combating the encreasing influence of the Crown, it was the intrigues of Carlton House counteracting the intrigues of St. James's. Were I asked to personify the Genius of the Party at that time I should say we had a thing presented to us, a bloated fantastical figure with a dice-box in one-hand, a goblet in the other, her cheeks flaming with drunkenness, the contending passions of Avarice and Lust glaring fiercely in her bewildered

D eyes ;

eyes ; the Cap of Liberty, indeed, ftill half placed and tottering on her head ; and Magna Charta torn and trodden at her feet.

The puppet-fhew of patriotifm was ftill exhibited to us, but we paffed filently and fcornfully by.—The zealous enthufiafm difplayed at your convivial meetings, communicated not itfelf to the dejected breafts of the people.—The caufe of liberty became degraded whilft ferving but to give a zeft to your wine, and evaporating in the quaintnefs of a toaft.

Whilft furveying you as the head of a once refpectable oppofition, the memory of your paternal Grandfather forcibly occurs to me.—Like you, Sir, he oppofed the Adminiftration of his time,—but here the fimilitude is concluded : He added dignity and refpect where you have diffeminated difgrace. Accufe me not, Sir, of an invidious diftinction if I dwell with a longing fatisfaction on the conduct of this amiable man. With abilities neither great by nature nor much improved

proved by education, he conducted himself
with a propriety your moſt daring panegy-
riſts would not be hardy enough to aſcribe to
you.—Unable, perhaps, to reaſon upon duties in the Abſtract, he, nevertheleſs, prac-
tiſed them in the detail.—With a mind little
calculated to develope the intricacies of political ſcience, the goodneſs of his heart in-
ſtinctively led him to embrace certain great
leading principles, which Reaſon alſo whiſ-
pered him were right. Gentle by nature,
and anxious to promote the happineſs of mankind, he had ſagacity enough to diſcover that
no means could be better ſuited to ſo virtuous
an end than the evincing his attachment to
the cauſe of liberty ; and in this purſuit he
was uniformly conſtant to the hour of his
death. It was this Prince of Wales who,
when the ſcantineſs of his income rather than
his ſhameleſs extravagance, had involved him
in pecuniary diſtreſs, and who, when he was
urged to make an application to Parliament,
virtuouſly exclaimed " that he would ſuffer
any hardſhip rather than add to the burthens
of an honeſt and indulgent people."

The

The country was not then infulted with the mock parade of retrenchment, whilft the fecret fprings of expence were ftill continuing to move with unabated power.

It was this Prince of Wales who, retiring not with fullen difdain and contumelious reproaches, but with the cheerful confcioufnefs of virtue; carried with him the efteem and confidence of the nation. They faw his little court, glorious in its humility, affording an afylum to genius, to learning, and to virtue. The Egalitès and the Barrymores of the age gave way to the more diftinguifhed names of a Mallet, a Thompfon, and a Glover. The verfatility of your character, your comprehenfive fcale of action from the meridian of the court to the mephitic atmof-phere of the gaming-houfe, render you an admirable fubject for the fpeculations of the comparative hiftorian. Some, perhaps, more pedantically malignant than myfelf, would fancy they could recognize in your conduct the taftelefs debaucheries of a Clodius; the groffer fenfualities of a Tarquin; and the

ftupid

ftupid buffoonery of a Nero. But I fpare you, Sir, the unmerited mortification of fuch degrading comparifons. I will for a moment forget what you are, and endeavour to explain to you what you are not: whilft I deteft the fallacy of a very popular prejudice, evidently of a dangerous tendency, and which feems not a little to have fanctioned, in your own opinion, the various exceffes of your life.—— Your advocates, who, though afhamed of your conduct, ftill were unwilling to abandon you to general difgrace, have often attempted to fhelter your irregularities under a refemblance, they affected to fay, you bore to a perfon of high celebrity in the annals of this country.—The name of HENRY V. cannot but be familiar to you. The heterogeneous character of this extraordinary man renders him a moft infinuating and dangerous object of imitation. He was, in an eminent degree, an inftance of the "*Exemplar vitiis imitabile*," as expreffed by HORACE, fo feductive to the indifcriminating minds of youth.—Hiftory has rarely prefented to us a perfon on whom virtus   i vice have been fo peculiary blended. It is by fuch characters even the cautious feverity of wifdom is beguiled of its frown, and involuntarily foothed into an approbation of the moft undignified follies:—It is thus the odium excited by Henry's propenfities to illiberal pleafures, has been forgotten in the admiration of his princely heroifm. Such, Sir, is the man you would be thought to refemble; for you have not efcaped the infidious flattery of thofe who, whilft they found a fimilarity in your early vices, hoped, or pretended to hope, for an equal participation of virtue. If he really be the model you have afpired to equal, we cannot give you much credit for the clumfy imitation:—We ftart at the rude, mifhapen, and imperfect outline; but look in vain for the mafterly touches, the bewitching graces, the bold and expreffive beauties of the fplendid original. Like Henry, Sir, you have had your Falftaffs, your Bandolphs, and your Piftols, lefs witty, perhaps, than the joyous fpirits of Eaftcheap, but of lives equally depraved and immoral:—Even in the choice of your companions, where

you

you approach neareſt to the captivating Henry, we are unwillingly obliged to con- feſs your inferiority. Amidſt the diſorderly ſtupidity, the taſteleſs abſurdities that cha- racteriſe your daily feſtivities, we diſcover none of thoſe ſprightly ſallies, thoſe irreſiſt- ible flaſhes of humour that were wont to en- liven the revels of the hero of Agincourt.— Should there be any "prickt to it by fooliſh honeſty and love," ſo miſtakenly kind as to keep alive a compariſon which, however plauſible in the infancy of your exceſſes, muſt now riſe up to whelm you in confu- ſion, let ſuch men remember, that the early youth of Henry was diſtinguiſhed by a firm and ardent attention to the duties of his ſi- tuation : that it was not 'till the jealouſy of his father had excluded him from the proper exerciſe of his active talents, that he ſought employment in the outrages of intemperate pleaſure.—Let them remember with what ſplendour he at intervals emerged from the clouds of impurity that encircled him : that he lived to realize the hopes of an admiring nation—hopes not haſtily formed upon vague

and

and ill-adapted comparifons, but infpired and invigorated by thofe rays of virtue which fo frequently burft from the general darknefs of his conduct. Let them remember that, with a mind irritated by the fatigues and horrors of an hazardous warfare, he difdained not the tendernefies of pure and honourable love ; and (which, Sir, may a little excite your aftonifhment) that the mild and affectionate duties of an hufband and a father were not forgotten in the turbulent avocations of the Hero. Laftly, Sir, let your advocates remember that, at a period of life, not more advanced than that to which you have arrived, and in which you now ftand before us a caufe of mourning to the country,

" *Wherein thou lieft in reputation fick,*"

the illuftrious Henry terminated a reign of the moft dazzling glory.

Praife in the fervice of fuch men, ceafes to be proftitution—it becomes a duty—it partakes of the divine qualities attributed to Mercy—

" It

"It blefficth him that gives and him that takes."

Every thing which in its performance is a virtue, is proportionably in its violation a crime. What then fhall I fay to the fallen mind of that man who hails you as the " pride and glory of the nation ?*" Little caufe as you have given me to awaken my compaffion, I really pity you, Sir, the mortification you muft feel from fuch humiliating flattery. If the circumftance could fail to be attended with the keen and agonizing reflection of what you once were and what you now are, I could imagine you laughing at your fublime panegyrift :—Yes, Sir, you laugh in very bitternefs, you deride him in the fulnefs of your fcorn.

Shall we fuffer our honeft indignation to cry aloud, or fhall we filently give vent to our tears, when we behold a man, once foremoft in the ranks of liberty, who has animated us by his zeal, and inftructed us by

---

* See Mr. Burke's Letters.

E   his

his wifdom; on whofe eloquence we have hung with rapture; who has ftrewed the paths of Philofophy with rofes, degraded to the fawning and penfioned advocate of Royalty. At that period of life when the intemperance of paffion, the refentments of injuries ufually ceafe to be remembered; when they fubfide into univerfal benevolence; when the mind dwells with anguifh on the flighteft wrong it may have occafioned, and fighs for inftant reparation; at fuch a moment fhall we endure to behold him tottering on the verge of annihilation, with his laft breath kindling the expiring embers of that flame that has already defolated Europe? Is the furious bigotry of opinion to be glutted and appeafed but with the blood of thoufands and tens of thoufands? Have we recoiled with a mixture of horrour and unbelief at the reported ferocity of the dying imprecations of the *Iroquois* and *Illenois*; and fhall we not fhudder at the barbarous fanaticifm of the vifionary politician who, in the laft convulfive ftruggle of his difordered being, aims a deadly blow at the happinefs of mankind

and

and who, like Sampſon, buries himſelf in the bloody trophies of his refiftlefs ftrength.

Pardon me, Sir, for having quitted you ſo long.—I return to condole with you on the ſhame that muſt overwhelm you whilſt you receive the diſgraceful flattery of this "foolifh fond old man."—I leave him to admire, with phrenzied delight, the high-wrought decorations, the luxuriant foliage of the *Capitals* of " the *Corinthian pillars* of the *State* :"—Mine be the humbler yet more valuable employment, by cleanſing the deceitful rubbiſh heaped around their baſe, to deteċt their latent weakneſs, and ſecure their trembling foundations.

Not to fatigue myſelf with the detail of circumſtances comparatively of ſmall importance when oppoſed to thoſe I am about to notice, I ſhall paſs over in ſilent diſdain the petty enumeration of your unmanly pleaſures. Let the grooms of Newmarket, the ſcene-ſhifters of the Theatres, the menials of thoſe in whoſe polluted embraces you have

wantoned

wantoned, glory in having witneffed the paftimes of degraded Royalty :—Let them enjoy the coarfe fneer ;—let them brood over the wretched confolation of beholding the Prince reduced to a level with themfelves :— your example may be of fervice to them :— their minds, un-educated as they are, may yet comprehend, from the view of your humiliating ftate, that nothing is really, refpectable but Virtue.

The year 1788 was diftinguifhed by an event which no one regarded with indifference, however varioufly it might have affected the feelings of individuals. Out of the fphere of politics, (if fuch an event indeed could be feparated from political confiderations) one fentiment of general forrow operated on every breaft. Awfully and filently as the fpeculative philanthropift might weep over the calamities incident to humanity, or ponder on the inftability of earthly greatnefs, far different were the vehement emotions that convulfed the political world on this important occafion

"an

" ————— an univerſal hubbub wild,
Of ſtunning ſounds and voices all confuſed."
PAR. LOST.

Never was a political conteſt conducted
with more indecent and illiberal warmth.
It was now, Sir, that the maſk was entirely
removed from the party of which you pro-
feſſed to be at the head. The intemperate
eagerneſs with which they graſped at the
tottering crown of their amiable and unhappy
Sovereign, the ferocious ſmile of exultation
that ſullenly gleamed amidſt the tears they
affected to ſhed for his miſery, told us but
too plainly that with them patriotiſm had
ſerved but as the cloak of diſappointed ambition ; that their former energy in the cauſe
of the people was without ſincerity, as their
preſent avidity of power was without decency, without principle. To thoſe who
could reſtrain their ſorrowfu! indignation, it
muſt have afforded matter of infinite ridicule
to obſerve the aukward inconſiſtency of thoſe
rien, who had, a few hours before, been
loudeſt in the cauſe of liberty ; the terror of
Miniſters ;

Minifters; the correctors of the. Royal prerogative, fuddenly, as if fome mifchievous
Fairy* had inverted their eye-lids, madly
doating on the object of their former difguft.—
The fidelity of the beft hearts towards their
humiliated Sovereign, trembled in fearful
equilibrium. The bulletin of dawning con-
valefcence, or returning malady, alternately
operated on the doubtful fcale.

The eager and unqualified expreffions of
attachment you received from a neighbouring
kingdom, the inebriate ardor with which they
conferred upon you the exercife of Royal Authority, flattering as it might be to the fuper-
ficial conclufions of your vanity, could have
occafioned but trifling exultation in the breafts
of confiderate politicians of your party.—Un-
eafinefs at their own miferable government;
a love of any change infeparable from every
ftate whofe vital principles are choaked with
corruption, were the motives that actuated

---

* See Midfummer Night's Dream.

the

the people of Ireland to fo precipitate a meafure.—They were prompted by

" *No love of thee or thine.*"
COWPER.

It was not confidence in you, but diffatisfac-
tion with themfelves : it was the reftlefs
turbulence of difeafe rather than the tempe-
rate energy of health.

If I am difpofed to cenfure your deviation
from political decency at this calamitous period, how little lenity can you expect from
me when I hear of your fpurning men at the
almoft irrefiftible impulfe of natural affection*. The page of hiftory is, indeed,
blotted by the memorials of men who have
allowed the ambition of power to triumph
over the beft and tendereft affections of Na-

---

* I know not well how to give credit to certain Tales of the
vifits of affected condolance and enquiry at W———r having
afforded a fubject for mimiekry and raillery in the convivial
parties at C———n H———e. For the credit of human nature
I hope the affertion is falfe—as for myfelf I *cannot* believe it.

ture :

ture : but thefe inftances are rare, and have occurred in times, comparatively fpeaking, of imperfeét civilization. I blufh, Sir, to have it recorded that in thefe days of refined and enlightened knowledge, there fhould have lived a man who, in the petty charac- ter of the intriguing politician, was forgetful of the facred offices of filial duty : that your affociates, needy by their exceffes, hardened by intemperance, with ambition maddened almoft to phrenzy by reftraint, fhould have violently rufhed to the banquet, from which they had fo long been withheld, was no extraordinary occurrence to thofe who were accuftomed to refleét on the operations of the human paffions.——But the hand of Heaven, which had humbled our Sovereign, as your verfatile panegyrift exultingly exclaimed*, to a fituation which the meaneft cottager muft furvey with compaffionate pity, was fuddenly ftretched forth in our defence. The return- ing health of your father, whom you had fo

---

* See Mr. Burke's Speeches on the Regency.

unworthily

unworthily treated, whofe forrows, fo far
from having awakened that fpirit of humanity that was fuppofed to inhabit your breaft,
feemed only to have aroufed the moft intemperate affections, fhone on our night of dif-
quiet, and reftored to us the fun-fhine of
confidence and peace.—You and your affociates fullenly retired, baffled and confounded,
from the inglorious ftruggle, a memorable
example of difappointed ambition, uncheered
by one comfortable reflection, unaccompa-
nied with one figh, except from thofe whofe
temporizing avarice had withdrawn them
from the banners of grateful and affectionate
loyalty.

Your character, Sir, is marked by too
many great and prominent characteriftics to
allow me to wafte much time in elucidating
its minutiæ.—I forbear to trifle with the numerous finer ramifications of folly ; I wifh to
aim a furer blow at its principal and leading
branches. The fubjects of your debts have
been fo forcibly and fo ably treated by a wri-
ter of acknowledged ability, that I forbear to

F   trefpafs

trefpafs much on your time in the difcuffion
of this degrading topic. Twice have we beheld you reduced to a ftate of the moft humiliating infolvency :—we have feen you
imploring the affiftance of an indignant, yet
relenting Parliament in the moft abject terms :
—we have heard your vows of repentance,
and your premifes of reform : and we have
lived to fee thofe vows and thofe promifes
violated and forgotten.—We have contem-
plated, with a fenfation of pity, your princely dignity virtually fubjected to all the rude
and unmannerly proceffes of a common bankruptcy. Whilft the motley group of your
creditors poured in their claims to the Com-
miffioners appointed to liquidate your debts ;
whilft the band of your needy dependents,
jewellers, trinket merchants, tavern-keepers,
and proftitutes, thronged unblufhingly round
your gates, could we have difcovered, apart
from the rapacious crowd, *one* half-retiring,
one blufhing yet meekly confident individual,
whofe merits or whofe misfortunes alone had
rendered him a claimant on your bounty, a
fentiment of virtuous delight would have
tempered

tempered our refentment, and where we now
reluctantly condemn, we fhould have haft-
ened to applaud.—But alas ! Sir, fuch items
of benevolent indifcretion are not to be found
in the lengthened column of your debts—the
gloomy catalogue is compofed of very different materials :—Every variety of effeminate
luxury ; the expences of undignified pleafures ; bonds and fecurities haftily and pro-
fufely granted as a temporary relief from
heavy debts unworthily contracted ; immenfe
fums lavifhed to fupport the exiftence of the
little *ephemera* of nobility, who fluttered in
the fun-fhine of your favour : fuch, Sir,
were the ingredients of the unfeemly mafs of
corruption, which, fwelling and gathering
to a head, burft into ruin.

There is one circumftance fo intimately
connected with that part of my fubject immediately in queftion, that I cannot avoid no-
ticing it in this place ;—I mean, your attachment to a woman on whom, by your attentions, you conferred a confiderable degree of
notorious celebrity :—I ufe this qualifying

expreffion

expreffion from a fenfation of caution infpired by the myftery that envelopes the whole of this extraorainary tranfaction. I fhould be as unwilling to wound the fuffering delicacy of injured virtue, as I fhould fpurn at the idea of refcuing vice from the falutary difcipline of cenfure; but conjecture would, in this inftance, be cruel as it is unneceffary. I fhudder to tear open wounds but yet imperfectly healed. The object of your former devotion, as fhe is now removed from the world, is equally infenfible perhaps to its praifes and its cenfures.—If her love for you was criminal, fhe is atoning for her error by a life of humiliating repentance.—If her bofom is free from the remorfeful recollection of a paffion fhe was taught perhaps to confider as virtuous; if fhe carries with her the applaufes of a pure and unfullied confcience, fhe is in the poffeffion of that before which the pomp of palaces finks into nothing. When confidering the fubject as applying folely to yourfelf, pardon me, Sir, if I difmifs my fenfitive delicacy.—The queftion inftantly refolves itfelf into this fimple alternative:

native : *you were her husband—or you were not.* You are in a dilemma, and, indeed, a very unfortunate one ; but as it is my intention to reject every kind of courtly accommodation in the developement of truth, to discipline and not to soothe you into virtue, I shall treat you with unceremonious frankness.

That you were actually married to the lady in question according to the laws of this country, that you subjected yourself to the indissoluble ties of a legal engagement, never, I believe, was suspected even by those who best knew your impatience of impediments in the gratification of your passions.—But, Sir, there are other tribunals to which we are amenable, independent of those established for the protection of human laws—There is an appeal to Honor; an appeal to Humanity; an appeal to Conscience.—It is one thing to steer cautiously within the pale of the written law, and to exclaim with the malignant satisfaction of a Shylock—" Is it in the Bond ?" But it is another thing to
obey

obey the unwritten dictates of that internal
fenfe of virtue, which rifes fuperior to the
fetters of artificial obligation, whofe nature is
too fubtle to be reducible to rule, and whofe
now ftill fmall voice fhall plead thunder-
tongued before the throne of Eternal Juftice.

Oh Sir, "lay not the flattering unction to
your foul."—Whatever plaufible and fophif-
tical chicaneries may have been exerted;
whatever ingenious falvos may have been fa-
bricated; whatever opiates you may have adminiftered, to lull the confcience of the object of your affections; however you may
have clipped and filed the ordinances of the
Church; however you may have half-mut-
tered and mutilated its ceremonies; ftill, if
you allowed the impreffion to operate on her
mind that fhe was virtually your wife, you
are *bona fide* at this moment her hufband.—
Your conduct would, in fuch a cafe, indeed
be immaculate to the un-microfcopic eye of
the law—but

" ————— *'tis not fo above—*
" *There is no fhuffling: there the action lies*
" *In its true nature.—*" HAMLET.

Should

Should you ftand acquitted of an offence, of which common charity induces me to fuppofe you guiltlefs, it remains that I immediately advert to the only alternative that prefents itfelf:—To plead one error in extenuation of another, is but an humiliating mode of defence; but fuch as it is I accept it, and will meet you on fair and candid grounds. I take it for granted, that you prudently preferred fimple concubinage to more ferious and fatiguing engagements :—fuch a method of indulging your defires you perhaps thought, from comparatively reafoning, would have but few inconveniences :—perfect freedom would not only relieve you from the horrors of enflaved fatiety, but would rather prolong the feafon of enjoyment ; and when your idol fhould fail in her attractions, it would be but exercifing a more than ufual fhare of your extravagant bounty, and the affair would be quietly difpofed of as though it had never been.—Such is the plaufible reafoningof fome men who never want an argument to perfuade themfelves of the expediency of any meafure likely to contribute to their
pleafure

pleafure—and I believe, Sir, it was yours—
indeed the confequences have proved it.   The
Lady has retired from your inconftant embraces with a quietus of 4000l. a year.—I am
almoft unwilling to ruffle the calm and com-
placent fatisfaction you feel whilft contem-
plating the facility with which great minds
rife fuperior to the moft trying fituations.—
How dexteroufly, with what a fimple ope-
ration have you out-leapt all the barriers of
moral obligation ;—with what princely compofure do you change your miftrefles ; with
the fame eafe as your fubjects would change
their clothes !   How magically, with a fingle ftroke of your pen, have you reinftated
yourfelf into the ineftimable liberty of gratifying unfettered, your next fantaftic inclination.   We could, indeed, furvey with admiration the rapid machinery, the exquifite
theatrical effect with which you introduce and
convey your puppets from the ftage : but we
are alarmed by the coftly expence of your ap-
paratus.—For one fingle movement in the
fcene,

   4000l. a year ! ! !

             On

On fuch a fubject it becomes me to be ferious.—As virtue and vice feem to have been adopted in the infant ftate of fociety, as names for fuch things as were found to be ufeful or prejudicial to its general or minuter interefts; and as it appears that the excellence and heinoufnefs of each were eftimated proportionably as their properties were extenfive, or their ramifications of confequent good and evil became multiplied, it is the duty of a moralift not merely to confider every action in its fimple and uncompounded fenfe, and to look not beyond its nominal definition, but to calculate its moft diftant effects, and to examine all its relative bearings on the commom interefts of mankind — From this confideration I might be expected not merely to regard the connexion in queftion fimply as a criminal indulgence of paffion, but that I fhould difcriminate all the gathering minutiæ of evil.—But I muft claim an exemption from the utmoft rigours of my duty, and be allowed to forbear particularizing each accumulated aggravation, whilft I reft

G   folely

folely on the laſt ſhameful conſequence of this diſgraceful tranſaction.

That in the moment of univerſal calamity, whilſt we are trembling on the verge of a national bankruptcy, whilſt we are deluged with taxes, little ſhort of total confiſcation ; whilſt the hard-earned wages of the poor and induſtrious peaſantry are barely ſufficient to ſupply the common neceſſaries of life, there ſhould live a man who throws the munifi-- cent bounty of the nation into the vortex of folly and diſſipation, is a reflexion that calls a tear from the eye of Humanity, and bids the cheek of Juſtice kindle with reſentment. I ſhall, perhaps, be inſultingly told, that every one has the liberty of appropriating his own money ;—but beware, Sir, of too haſ-- tily availing yourſelf of the dangerous prin-- ciple—there is treachery in the poſition— the money you ſquander is the money of the people—it is the fruit of their labour and their bounty :—it is from them you receive it, and it is to them you muſt render an ac-- count.—It will, no doubt, awaken your in-- dignation ;

dignation; but know, Sir, there is not a poor mechanic who drags out his comfortlefs exiſtence in his miſerable garret, or a menial porter tottering under his burthen in the ſtreets of the metropolis, to whom you are not indebted for ſome ſhare of your ſplendid luxuries.

I will give you pauſe to ruminate on this bitter and unqueſtionable truth.——I will exclaim, in the pathetic language of the humilitated LEAR,

> " *Take phyſic Pomp;*
> " *Expoſe thyſelf to feel what wretches feel.*"

And may you, Sir, by reflecting on the miſeries and poverty of two-thirds of your benefactors, learn a better uſe of the bleſſings of proſperity.

I now approach, Sir, the moſt important æra of your life : an æra which, as it opened to us the proſpect of beholding you emanci-

pated

pated from the fhackles of folly, was hailed
with unufual fatisfaction.—It was now that
the prophetic predictions of your fome time
ftarting with virtuous fplendour, were regarded as accomplifhed.—Your infpired panegyrifts, whom no difaftrous omens had
ever difconcerted, were now feen in every
circle fwelling with proud and confcious exultation. You heroically refolved to be virtuous, and you felected as an affociate in this
amiable purpofe, one who, whatever might
be the pure and exalted pleafures of an inno-
cent and honorable life, would, by her participation of them, communicate an encreafing
luftre and a ten-fold fweetnefs.—Your firft
approaches to virtue were mixed with a little
degree of waywardnefs, which did not, however, difcourage us from hoping to witnefs
your complete reformation. Bad and inve-
terate habits are not conquered in a day ; and
it could hardly be expected that you fhould
abandon thofe fantaftic pleafures, in whofe
embraces you had wantoned from your youth,

" *Nor caft one longing-lingering look behind.*"

But

But when the hour arrived that made you the hufband of a lovely, accomplifhed, and virtuous woman, a princefs and your near relation, it was believed that you and your vices were to be feparated for ever.—But, good God, Sir, how fhall I exprefs to you the univerfal fenfation of indignant aftonifhment, when " not one little month" from the time when, in the face of the World, in the face of Heaven, you pledged yourfelf to love, to honour, and to cherifh this amiable ftranger as your wife, we beheld you loft to fhame, to virtue, and to humanity, turning coldly from the tender and affectionate offices of an hufband, and rioting in the admiration of faded and antiquated beauty !

What a mournful picture of fuffering virtue and intriguing profligacy did your family prefent to the eyes of an infulted nation !— With what compofure could they behold your Princefs bathed in her tears, expofed to the infolent merriment of her fervants, whom

your

your favor had intoxicated, and your follies had corrupted, hourly compelled to receive the infidious attentions of a malignant rival, the fubject of your farcaftic ridicule, the victim of your fullen fpleen?—How could they bear to know that fuch was the fituation of a woman, whom, with the natural generofity of Englifhmen, they had hailed with tranfport, and whofe happinefs they confidered as a facred depofit entrufted to their hands?

I become faint and difpirited whilft I endeavour to trace the accumulated wickednefs, the malicious refinements, the endlefs gradations of cruelty, that have been exercifed on this lovely and unfortunate ftranger.—No, Sir, it was not enough that your palace was become to her the dungeon of defpair rather than the abode of domeftic tranquility, but even the external fources of comfort, to which fhe might fly for a momentary confolation, were poifoned and corrupted.—Methinks I fee her turning to the few of her countrywomen whom your policy conde-

fcended

fcended to allow to remain about her perfon, and exclaiming

Alas ! poor wenches ! where are now your
     fortunes ?
Shipwreck'd upon a kingdom where no pity,
No friends, no hope, no kindred weep for
     me ;
Almost no grave allowed me.——
         HENRY VIII.

The minds of your whole family were to be perverted by your infidious artifices.—— The virtuous Daughter-in-law was treated with cold and unfeeling indifference, whilft the painted image of difgrace fluttered in the courtly circle, covered with careffes—

    O fhame, fhame, fhame ! ! !

But the Royal protection of fuch indecorum was too feeble to refift the tide of popular refentment. The people were not to be fneeringly chilled or haughtily frowned into an oblivion

vion of the beſt affections of nature.—They had imbibed their ideas of moral rectitude from other and purer ſources than from the worldly and ſophiſticated codes of Courts. It became neceſſary now, Sir, for the faction that was leagued to deſtroy the happineſs of this unfortunate Princeſs, and againſt whom the bitterneſs of one, though a ſmall part of the community ſeemeed, to encreaſe proportionally with the compaſſion of the other, to adopt at leaſt ſomething like the apppearance of atonement—The countenance of your parents was for a moment withdrawn —a ſcene of pretended indignation immediately ſucceeded : a reform was inſtituted in your houſehold : ſome odious characters were removed becauſe they could no longer be kept, and with the beſt grace you could afſume, though not without much ſeeming reluctance, you coldly pronounced *A Reconciliation.*

For once in your life, Sir, you ſacrificed a little to appearance—A ſolemn meeting was appointed,

appointed, your weeping and much injured Princefs met you with looks of affectionate forgivenefs, and the world believed you to *repent*—But let me not prophane the expreffion by ufing it on fo unworthy an occafion—The temporizing and licentious Commodus repented but to take breath for more inordinate gratifications.

Is it in the formal ceremonies of a ftate dinner, is it in one day, perhaps in a month fnatched from your fecret indulgencies with your former creatures, and freezingly dedicated to ill-counterfeited attentions to your wife, is it in a life of almoft total feparation, in the abborrence of all domeftic enjoyments, in an hardened indifference to your child, that we are to recognize repentance and reconciliation?

Think not, Sir, that fo flimfy a veil can conceal this glaring outrage to decency— Where are we to look for thofe tender attentions, that interchange of fentiment, that union of pleafure, that fympathy of feeling

H which

which in more humble life would be regarded as the inevitable confequences of a pure and perfect reconciliation ?—I know of no Royal exemption from the common feelings of human nature, nor do I know of any princely prerogative in the eftimating of moral duties. —Your illuftrious Confort will feel her injuries as a woman : and as a man your conduct is amenable to the ftandard of common juftice.

Thefe are not times, Sir, to trifle with the affections of the people and to diffipate thofe rays of facred opinion which, to ufe the words of your elegant preceptor " are the real ftrength as well as the gilding of the Crown."—It is in vain we pour the thunders of eloquence, and level the ordnance of power againft the accumulating forces of Revolutionifm ; it is in vain we rudely tear the faireft bloffoms from the garland of Liberty, if we ftoop not to apply an antidote to that infidious poifon, which creeping to the very vitals of the conftitution, threatens a flow but inevitable death.—He would be regarded as an ignorant Empiric, who whilft endeavour-ing to ftrengthen his patient againft the ima-ginary approaches of a dangerous diforder, fhould fuffer a latent difeafe to rankle in his frame and gather into mortality—If the ge-nius of republicanifm is abroad, and threatens injury to our conftitution, let us examine its minuteft defects, let us difcover its moft vulnerable parts; let its breaches be healed and its weakneffes be ftrengthened—To hate Republicans let us firft learn to love our Princes; let Jacobinical vices be oppofed by Royal virtues. We are now, Sir, in the fifth year of a war, which, for the injuftice of its origin, the camelion-like diverfity of its object, the blind and obftinate pertinacity with which it has been conducted, the cala-mity and bloodfhed with which it has been marked, is unparalleled in the annals of this country.—We have beheld a war in whofe defence the name of every thing facred has been proftituted to ftimulate us, to which the richeft ftores of our language have been ex-haufted, covering us with fhame and confu-

H 2

fion—

fion—It is in vain that our calculators and our ftatefmen have penetrated the depths of political fcience, and proved from eftablifhed data the ruin of our enemies, it is vain the puny dependants of Minifters have fatigued us with the frothy declamations of their fchools, annihilating armies with the lightening of a metaphor and the majefty of a period—It is in vain the mild fpirit of Chriftianity has been goaded to aroufe our mind to the agonizing fcenes of flaughter and defolation—It is in vain we have been impioufly told the avenging hand of the Deity was ftretched out in our defence, that we were the chofen Minifters of his wrath.—The God we have fo daringly prophaned, has humbled us to the duft.

That a new political fyftem, fo decifive in its operations, plaufible, as it originated in the principles of reafon, captivating as it adminiftered to the miferies of an oppreffed people, fhould have excited the jealous fufpicions of the continental Courts, is not to be be wondered at—By governments founded on delufion and fupported by terror, the French Revolution could not be regarded with the eye of indifference—The light of Reafon and Philofophy burfting through the gloomy caverns of defpotifm, whilft it flafhed conviction on the ftubborn minds of the potentates of Europe, roufed them to a fatal and rancorous refentment—However local and confined the views of the new reformers might have been in the outlet of the revolution, The oppofition of Europe, by extending their views, armed their refolution and invigorated their zeal—It now became the facred ftruggle between Liberty and Defpotifm, and the impulfe of enthufiafm naturally infpired by the caufe of the former, has been irrefiftible—The fineft troops, the moft experienced Generals in the world, have returned baffled and defeated—If the narrow and ungenerous policy of crufhing a ftate in the moment of its weaknefs and diftraction, actuated the Continental powers in fo early declaring war againft the Republic of France, they have paid dearly for their error.

Their

Their oppofition has confolidated that ftupendous political fabric on a foundation which
no time will ever be able to fhake.

If a benevolent and imprudent emotion of
pity for a diftreffed Sovereign was the fecret
fpring of this bloody crufade, let it be known,
that war and defolation are not the proper
engines to enforce the mild leffons of humanity. If principles were to be refifted and
attacked, it fhould have been by the only
means by which they can be fuccefsfully
oppofed, by the panoply of reafon and truth.
It is to little purpofe Kings have fortified
their dungeons, and have forged new chains,
new implements of oppreffion : the phan-
tom of opinion, darting athwart the fullen
horizon of Europe, fhaking ten thoufand me-
teors from her wings, fpurns at their impo-
tent controul.

Little as this country might be fuppofed
to be affected by the terrors of a French Revolution, we did not long efcape the conta-
gion of Germanic feelings—we rufhed into
the bloody coalition: It is needlefs to trace
the

the various artifices, the flimfy pretexts, that were conjured up by the ftate magicians to afford us a colourable excufe for plunging us into a difaftrous war. However Minifters may have fucceeded for a time in affociating their own wretched caufe with that of the Conftitution ; whatever plaufible delufion they may have practifed over the honeft and confiding minds of the country at large, that delufion is nearly at an end. Though we wake to mifery, it is better than the fleep of death. I believe, Sir, it is no longer doubted that the fecret terror of the influence of French principles, a dread of that fpirit of philofophical enquiry that is now trying the eftablifhments of Europe, were the real and difguifed motives that actuated Minifters to the adoption of this ruinous meafure. Little as the Conftitution in its native and original purity has to apprehend from the minuteft examination, it was not fo with its abufes. The encroachments of power, the abominations of office, the difeafed debility of the popular and reprefentative part of the Legiflature, fhrunk from the keen and fearching eye of enquiry.—The old ftate tricks were

now

now to be exhibited. " The cry of the Conftitution is in danger," was re-echoed from office to office till the whole nation, like the hares in the fable, trembled at the motion of their own bodies. Left we might recover too foon from this temporary alarm, a more defperate game was to be played.— The policy of Cæfar covered his attacks upon Roman liberty by the fplendid exhibition of beafts and gladiators. Whilft treafon fkulked within the walls of the Capitol, the Amphitheatres rung with the applauding aftonifhment of thoufands. —We have had a more dreadful fpectacle prefented to us :—the fenfe of leffer inconveniences has, indeed, been forgotten in the frightful contemplation of our countrymen perifhing in the field, or feftering under the blighting mildew of peftilence.—We have for a moment been ftartled out of ourfelves ; but remember, Sir, the time is approaching when the horrors we deplore will redound on the heads of their authors with a ten-fold vengeance.— Adverfity is the fchool of wifdom ; and if that ftupendous cloud that is flowly moving

over

over our heads, black with gathering deftruction, forbears this time to burft and de-
luge us with ruin, our awakened fagacity
will inftruct us not haftily to encounter fimi-
lar miferies in future.—It is in fuch a moment of general difmay, when we know not
to whom to look for protection, that I am
anxious to warn you, Sir, of your precarious
fituation. The habits of your undignified
life have deprived us of the hope of expecting
from you that confolatiou which, in the hour
of danger, a good Prince ought to be able to
adminifter to his people. Alas, Sir, you neither infpirit us by your virtues, foothe us by
your affection, nor arm us by your wifdom.—
We have put you in the fcale, and you are
found wanting. Were our views bounded
by your prefent fituation, we fhould fit down
perhaps in filent and mournful difappoint-
ment. But when we reflect that in a few
days, a few hours, nay, at the very moment
we are thinking of you, the hand of Heaven
may have placed you on the throne, we tremble between our duty and our reafon. Your
conduct, Sir, is a national concern. This is

I

an

an age when things begin to be valued for what they are, not what they feem.

It is in vain we have endeavoured to enlarge our conftructions of treafon ; that we have fettered fociety with new fhackles of authority ; that we have exerted our reafon and our eloquence againft the new philofophy, if our doctrines are contradicted by our example. There is a Jacobinifm more poifonous, more fubtle, more deadly, than all that can be collected from the dreams of Theorifts, or the harangues of Demagogues—it is the Jacobinifm of Princely vices.

Good God! Sir, what infatuation can have fo dulled your mind to a fenfe of the confequences of your inconfiderate life ?—Whilft the fpirit of re-publicanifm fcowls around our palaces, fhall you, reeling from your midnight banquet, place in her hand the weapon of deftruction ? If the wifdom of our anceftors has entailed upon us the peaceful poffeffion of an hereditary and limited monarchy, forbear, Sir, to leffon
our

our confidence in their prudence, and our
gratitude for their kindnefs. It is to you,
Sir, we look as to a man who, by the future
wifdom of his councils, is to reftore the pal-
fied profperity of a once great and flourifhing
kingdom.—It is on you we reft our hopes,
and *dare* not difappoint them. The Empe-
ror, the father of his people, ceafed to be
acknowledged by the Romans in the effeminate fon of Caracalla. Have we fought?
have we bled? are we poor? are we divided?
are we difgraced? We have ftill our Conftitution.—To whom are we to truft the in-
valuable treafure? If the review of a life
wifely and honourably fpent infpire you with
a virtuous confidence, ftand forth, Sir, and
exclaim to an anxious nation—" *I am the*
Man!"

If you fhrink, I tremble for the confequences.

HAMPDEN.

F I N I S.

NEW PUBLICATIONS,

Printed for J. S. JORDAN, No. 166,
Fleet-Street.

LIFE OF CHARETTE.

This day was publifhed, price 1s. 6d.

MEMOIRS of CHARETTE, Chief of the Royal and Christian Armies, in the Interior of France; containing Anecdotes of the War in La Vendee.

By an Emigrant of Distinction.

Tranflated from the French.

London, printed for J. S. Jordan, No. 166, Fleet-ftreet.

Of whom may be had, price 2s. 6d.

THE FIVE MEN ; containing Memoirs and interefting Anecdotes of the prefent MEMBERS of the EXECUTIVE DIRECTORY of FRANCE—

BARRAS,	REWBELL,
CARNOT,	AND
LETOURNEUR,	LA REVELLIERE LEPAUX.

Tranflated from the French of Joseph Despaze,
By John Sodhart.

The avidity with which this work is at prefent read in Paris, together with the authenticity of its documents, and the impartiality of its principles, renders it one of the moft interefting productions to which the Revolution has given birth. It defcribes with energy and fidelity the collective operations of the Directory, as well as the particular Characters of the Individuals; and it is no lefs important from its political information, than from its biographical accuracy.

Alfo, Price 1s.

THREE LETTERS addreffed to the PEOPLE of GREAT BRITAIN, on the FAILURE of the LATE NEGOCIATION : including, a few HINTS on the Conduct proper to be adopted in the PRESENT SITUATION of AFFAIRS.

" Oh ! fhun that gulph, that gaping ruin fhun."—Thompson.

www.ingramcontent.com/pod-product-compliance
Lightning Source LLC
Chambersburg PA
CBHW021526090426
42739CB00007B/797